Picture the Past
Life at Ellis Island

Sally Senzell Isaacs

Heinemann Library
Chicago, Illinois

© 2002 Reed Educational & Professional Publishing
Published by Heinemann Library,
an imprint of Reed Educational & Professional Publishing,
Chicago, IL
Customer Service 888-454-2279
Visit our website at www.heinemannlibrary.com

Produced for Heinemann Library by
 Bender Richardson White.
Editor: Lionel Bender
Designer and Media Conversion: Ben White
Picture Researcher: Cathy Stastny
Production Controller: Kim Richardson

06 05 04
10 9 8 7 6 5 4 3

Printed in China

Isaacs, Sally Senzell, 1950-
 Life at Ellis Island / Sally Senzell Isaacs.
  p. cm. -- (Picture the past)
Includes bibliographical references (p.) and index.
 ISBN 1-58810-252-1 (hb. bdg.) ISBN 1-58810-417-6 (pbk.
bdg.)
 1. Ellis Island Immigration Station (N.Y. and N.J.)--
Juvenile literature. 2. Immigrants--Ellis Island (N.Y. and
N.J.)--Juvenile literature. 3. Ellis Island (N.J. and N.Y.)--
History--Juvenile literature. 4. United States--Emigration
and immigration--Juvenile literature. (1. Ellis Island
Immigration Station (N.Y. and N.J.)--History. 2. United
States--Emigration and immigration.) I.Title.
  JV6484 .I73 2001
  325.73--dc21
                                        2001000498

Special thanks to Mike Carpenter and Scott Westerfield at Heinemann Library for editorial and design guidance and direction, and to Jeff Dosik of the National Park Service at Ellis Island Immigration Museum for assistance in supplying photographic prints from original images.

Acknowledgments
The producers and publishers are grateful to the following for permission to reproduce copyright material:
By Courtesy of Ellis Island Immigration Museum: pages 1, 12, 15, 16, 18, 20, 21, 22, 24, 25. Corbis Images/Bettmann Archive: pages 13, 17, 23. Michael Yamashita/Corbis Images: page 30. North Wind Pictures: page 8, 19.
Cover photograph: By Courtesy of Ellis Island Immigration Museum.

Every effort has been made to contact copyright holders of any material reproduced in this book. Omissions will be rectified in subsequent printings if notice is given to the publisher.

Illustrations by John James, pages 26, 29; Gerald Wood, pages 7, 9.
Map by Stefan Chabluk.
Cover make-up: Mike Pilley, Radius.

Note to the Reader
Some words are shown in bold, **like this.** You can find out what they mean by looking in the glossary.

ABOUT THIS BOOK

This book tells about the life of the immigrants who passed through Ellis Island, New York, between 1892 and 1924. An immigrant is someone who comes from one country to live in a different country. There were other times in history when large groups of immigrants came to the United States. They include large groups of Europeans who started America's thirteen colonies. They also include the Africans who were forced to come as slaves. We have illustrated the book with photographs and drawings from this time period and with artists' ideas of how things looked then.

The Author
Sally Senzell Isaacs is a professional writer and editor of nonfiction books for children. She graduated from Indiana University, earning a B.S. degree in Education with majors in American History and Sociology. For some years, she was the Editorial Director of Reader's Digest Educational Division. Sally Senzell Isaacs lives in New Jersey with her husband and two children.

CONTENTS

Going to America

In the late-1800s, millions of people, from all over the world, wanted to live in the United States. They had heard that the United States had plenty of jobs, food, and, most of all, freedom. These people sold their belongings and left their homes forever. After traveling on crowded ships, they finally stopped at Ellis Island near New York City. Before they could go any further, **inspectors** and doctors on Ellis Island asked them questions, checked their health, and decided who could enter the United States and who could not.

Look for these
The illustration of the traveling boy and girl shows you the subject of each double-page story in the book.

The illustration of a steamship marks boxes with interesting facts about Ellis Island.

TIME LINE OF EVENTS IN THE DAYS OF ELLIS ISLAND

1892 Ellis Island opens.

1900 Ellis Island opens again with new brick buildings.

1917-18 During World War I, Ellis Island is used as an army hospital and place to hold captured German soldiers.

1890   1900   1910   1920   1930   1940

1897 Fire destroys all the buildings on Ellis Island.

1907 The busiest year: over one million people pass through Ellis Island.

1921 New law limits the number of **immigrants** allowed in the United States.

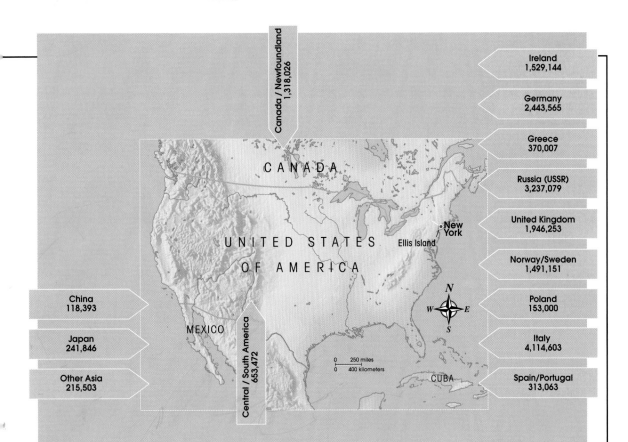

Canada / Newfoundland 1,318,026

Ireland 1,529,144

Germany 2,443,565

Greece 370,007

Russia (USSR) 3,237,079

United Kingdom 1,946,253

Norway/Sweden 1,491,151

Poland 153,000

Italy 4,114,603

Spain/Portugal 313,063

China 118,393

Japan 241,846

Other Asia 215,503

Central / South America 653,472

CANADA

UNITED STATES OF AMERICA

MEXICO

New York

Ellis Island

CUBA

0   250 miles
0   400 kilometers

More than twenty million people came to the United States between 1892 and 1924. About twelve million arrived at Ellis Island. Others landed in such cities as San Francisco, Boston, and Philadelphia. Many people stayed in these cities. Others rode trains to their new hometowns.

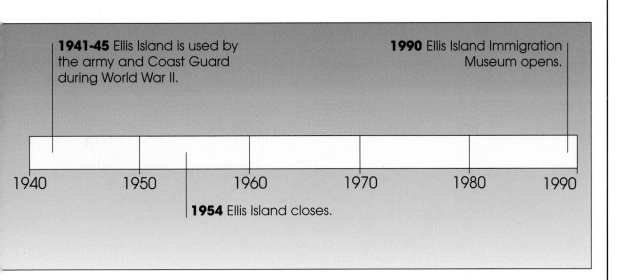

1941-45 Ellis Island is used by the army and Coast Guard during World War II.

1990 Ellis Island Immigration Museum opens.

1940   1950   1960   1970   1980   1990

1954 Ellis Island closes.

Leaving Home

In many countries, people were so poor that they could not feed their children. In other countries, people were punished because of their religions. Millions of these people heard stories about the United States. In the United States, people could practice a religion without fear. If they worked hard, one day they could buy a house and send their children to college.

These people are leaving Germany and going to the United States. They crowd onto a steamship. They probably do not understand English. They probably have little money.

Some families saved money for months or years to buy a ticket to the United States. Some people sold their watches. Some sold their silverware. Many families did not have enough money for everyone to travel. Often, the father left first. When he earned enough money in the United States, he sent tickets to his family.

WHERE THEY CAME FROM

The years 1892 to 1924 saw the largest movement of people in modern history.
• More than one million people came to the United States from Italy and Russia.
• More than 500 thousand people came from Hungary, Austria, Germany, England, and Ireland.
• More than 100 thousand people came from France, Poland, Sweden, Greece, Norway, Ottoman Empire, Scotland, the West Indies, and Portugal.

This family lives in England. The parents have lost their jobs. With no money, they cannot pay for their home. They hope for a better life in the United States.

Across the Ocean

Huge ships sailed from Europe. They were packed with people traveling to the United States. Many of these people were rich. They paid for private sleeping rooms and expensive food served in dining rooms.

Most **immigrants**—people coming to live in the United States—were poor. They paid for the cheapest tickets and stayed in **steerage,** which was like the basement of the ship.

The steerage section was very crowded. Everyone shared one bath area, which was often dirty and smelly. When one person got sick, the germs spread quickly.

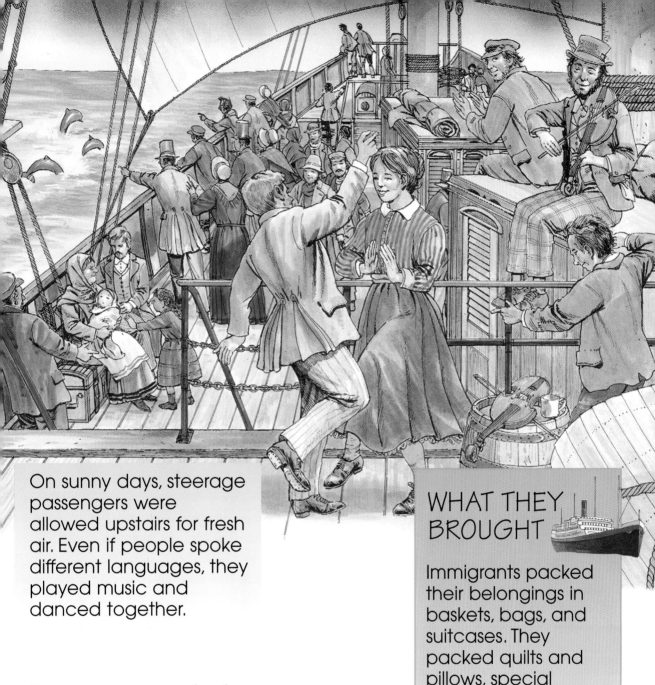

On sunny days, steerage passengers were allowed upstairs for fresh air. Even if people spoke different languages, they played music and danced together.

In steerage, people slept in rooms filled with bunk beds. Women and children slept in one room, men in another. Each person received a large spoon and tin pail to eat with on the entire trip. They ate boiled meat or soup for their meals. The food was often cold and tasted bad.

WHAT THEY BROUGHT

Immigrants packed their belongings in baskets, bags, and suitcases. They packed quilts and pillows, special dresses, books, and photographs. They wore several layers of clothes. Often they carried bread, cheese, and other food for the trip.

America!

The trip to the United States took between eight and fourteen days. Many days were stormy and the ship tossed from side to side. The **immigrants** were tired, hungry, and dizzy from **seasickness.** When the sun came out, everyone crowded outside on deck to watch for a sign of America. At last, they saw it—the Statue of Liberty.

After years of planning and days of traveling, the immigrants arrived in New York Harbor. Many people cried when they saw the Statue of Liberty. It stood for hope and freedom.

TICKET PRICES

A **steerage** ticket cost about $10 to $15. Today that is worth about $175 to $275.
Second-class passengers paid $30 to $35.
First-class passengers paid about $45.

The first-class and second-class passengers did not have to go to Ellis Island. **Inspectors** asked them a few questions on the ship. Then they were free to enter the United States. There were too many **steerage** passengers to talk to on the ship. They were taken to Ellis Island to answer questions.

First-class and second-class passengers are leaving the ship. Below them, the steerage passengers wait for smaller boats to arrive. The boats will take them to Ellis Island.

Ellis Island

These people are waiting for a smaller boat to take them from the ship to Ellis Island. Ellis Island is so busy that they may have to wait on the ship for several hours. Some people will wait several days.

When the small boats stopped, the **steerage** passengers could see their new country. The first place they saw was Ellis Island. There were no houses on the island, just buildings. Hundreds of people worked in the buildings. It was their job to check the new **immigrants** and help them get ready to enter the United States.

Ellis Island had 36 buildings. All the immigrants passed through the main building, called the Registry Building. The other buildings included hospitals, sleeping rooms, kitchen, dining room, laundry room, baggage room, library, post office, **telegraph** office, and railroad ticket office.

WORKERS

More than 500 people worked on Ellis Island. Some of their jobs were
- doctors and nurses
- **interpreters**
- **inspectors**
- office workers
- guards
- cooks
- painters
- baggage handlers

For most immigrants, Ellis Island was the first stop in the United States. Some immigrants called it the Island of Hope. Some called it the Island of Tears.

In the Past

Ellis Island did not always have 36 buildings. Hundreds of years ago, it had only trees and birds. **Native Americans** called it Kioshk, which means "Gull Island." In the 1600s, people called it **Oyster** Island. They had picnics there and collected oysters from the shore.

This is the main building on Ellis Island as it looked in 1938. It is built of bricks. The first buildings were made of wood and burned down in a fire in 1897.

In the 1700s, a man named Samuel Ellis owned the island and named it Ellis Island. When he died in 1807, the United States **government** bought the island. By 1890, thousands of **immigrants** were pouring into the United States. President Benjamin Harrison decided to turn Ellis Island into an **immigration center.**

This room is called the Great Hall. Here, in 1910, it is filled with hopeful immigrants. In 1911, the iron poles were taken out and replaced with more wooden benches.

Hope and Fear

Ellis Island became a very busy place. Every day, 3,000 to 5,000 people passed through the Great Hall. The tired **immigrants** looked around this strange, noisy place. People were talking in more than 30 different languages. They waited to be checked by doctors and to answer questions.

These immigrants are arriving at Ellis Island. They are carrying all their belongings with them.

Immigrants of all ages and from many different countries sit and stand in the waiting room on Ellis Island. An inspector stands in the back, watching them.

HEAVY LOAD

The immigrants carried their baggage inside the building. There, baggage handlers told them to leave it in a special room. Many people were afraid about losing their belongings. So they carried everything with them at all times.

The waiting immigrants shared the same thoughts: "Will I say the wrong thing? Will I fail the tests? Will the doctors find something wrong with me?" If things went smoothly, the immigrants could leave Ellis Island in a few hours. But some people had to stay longer to answer more questions. Some had to go to the hospital. Some were sent back home.

As the **immigrants** walked up the steps to the Great Hall, doctors watched them. They looked for trouble signs—breathing problems, limping, skin rashes. At the top of the steps, more doctors waited. They checked ears and eyes. If a doctor saw a problem, the person could not leave Ellis Island.

Doctors wanted to be sure that no immigrant brought a disease into the United States. They also wanted to be sure that an immigrant was strong enough to earn a living.

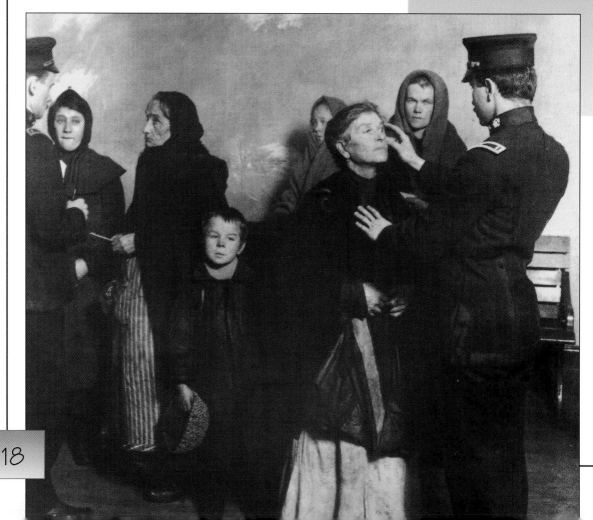

Next came the questions. **Inspectors** asked the immigrants questions. What is your name? Where are you going? What kind of work do you do? How much money do you have? Do you have relatives in the United States? Inspectors wanted to be sure the immigrants had a place to stay and enough money for a train ticket.

Interpreters stood beside the inspectors. They asked the questions in the immigrant's language. The immigrants had to read and write in their own languages. They also had to answer math problems.

CHALK MARKS

If doctors saw a problem, they marked a letter on the back of the immigrant's clothes. This person would be checked again. The letters were:

E for eye problem
L for lameness (walking problem)
F for rash on face
X for mental (thinking) problems
B for back problem
Sc for scalp problem

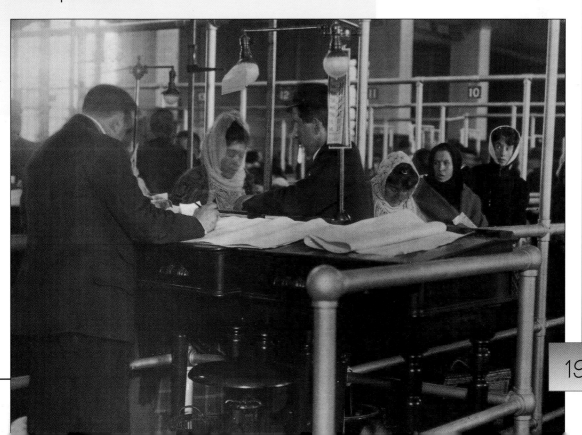

Stay or Leave?

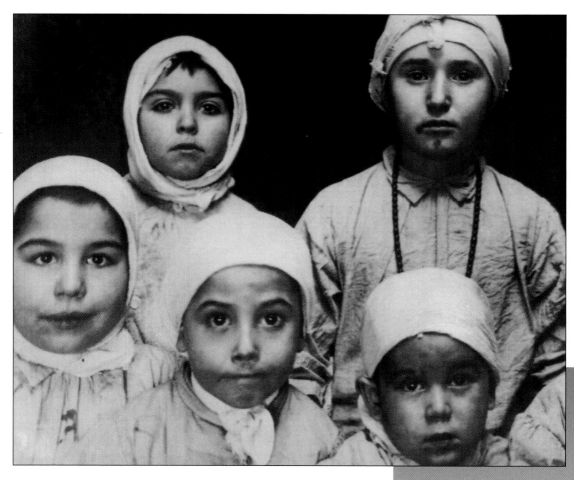

These children must stay on Ellis Island until they are well. They must stay in the hospital so other people do not catch their illnesses.

People who passed all the tests left Ellis Island in less than five hours. Some had to stay for days or weeks. Most people with diseases were sent to the hospital until they got better. People who failed the other tests had to wait for the **inspectors'** decision.

About 250 thousand people were sent back to their home countries. Some of these people were sent back because they had diseases and they would not get better. Others seemed to have no skills to get a job. Sometimes one member of a family was sent back while the others were allowed to enter the United States.

If one person in a family had to stay on Ellis Island, the other family members stayed, too. These children are playing in a roof garden while they wait.

STAYING AWHILE

Some **immigrants** who stayed on Ellis Island learned to speak English from the people who worked there. Children played games, sang songs, and listened to stories.

Eating and Sleeping

Sometimes more than 4,000 people slept on Ellis Island at once. The sick people stayed in hospitals. Their families slept in large rooms crowded with bunk beds. Each bunk had three stacked beds. The beds had no mattresses. People received two blankets, but they were often afraid to use them. The blankets seemed dirty and filled with bugs.

NEW CITIZENS

About 355 babies were born on Ellis Island. Because they were born in the United States, they were United States **citizens.**

There were about 725 hospital beds in Ellis Island. Between 1905 and 1914, there were fifteen medical buildings.

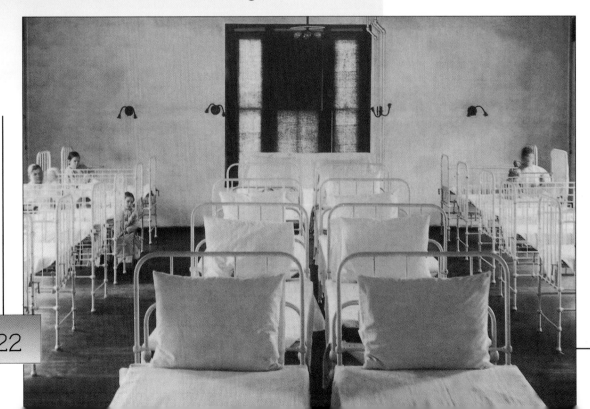

If immigrants stayed more than a few hours on Ellis Island, they were given a meal in the dining room. The room could seat 1,000 people.

People from different countries sat together in the dining room and tried to talk to one another. No matter what was served, it seemed strange to some of the people. Many **immigrants** had never eaten such things as oranges and bananas.

ON THE MENU

BREAKFAST: bread and butter, boiled eggs, coffee, milk
LUNCH: Beef stew, boiled potatoes
DINNER: Corned beef hash with green peppers, bread and butter, fruit

Leaving Ellis Island

After talking to doctors and **inspectors,** all the **immigrants** went down the "Staircase of Separation." People who did not pass the tests went straight ahead. They would sit in a waiting room to find out if they could stay for further examination. People who passed the tests received a "landing card." They now had permission to live in the United States!

These people have landing cards and have exchanged money from their home countries for American dollars. Workers at these windows will sell them railroad tickets.

The travel and waiting is over. These immigrants will soon be living in the United States. They are boarding boats that will take them from Ellis Island to New York City.

Many people planned to stay in New York City. Sometimes relatives came to meet them at Ellis Island. Other people bought train tickets to cities such as Boston and Pittsburgh. They went to the Ellis Island **telegraph** office and sent messages to their relatives to tell them what time their trains would arrive.

Work and School

Most **immigrants** were happy to work hard in the United States. Many took jobs in sewing factories. All day long, they stitched sleeves onto jackets or collars onto shirts. They worked ten to thirteen hours a day. Other immigrants helped build bridges, railroads, and buildings. Some opened barber shops, butcher shops, and shoe repair shops.

CHILDREN AT WORK

To help their families buy food, many children took jobs. The jobs included:
- selling flowers, newspapers, and candy
- running errands
- shining shoes
- working in factories

Many immigrants took jobs in America's busy car factories. In 1914, workers could put together a car in 90 minutes.

In the United States, children could go to school for free. Most immigrants wanted their children in school. It was hard for many immigrant children to learn anything because they did not understand English. After a while, the children learned the language. Then when their parents needed to talk to a doctor, landlord, or shopkeeper, the children were the **interpreters.**

Immigrants from the same country moved to the same neighborhoods. People from Poland lived in this neighborhood in Chicago.

Food

One hundred years ago, there were no large supermarkets. People walked down the street and bought meat from the butcher and vegetables from a farmer's cart. They bought cakes in the bakery and milk from a milkman. Most people did not have refrigerators. Several times a week, someone delivered a block of ice. Until the ice melted, it kept food cold.

These boys are selling bread on a sidewalk in New York City. People sold many things from carts. They sold fish, fruit, clothes, shoes, and brooms.

Immigrant's Recipe—Noodle Kugel

Immigrants cooked many recipes from their home countries. We still eat these foods today. This is a recipe for a sweet noodle pudding made by the Jewish immigrants from Eastern Europe.

WARNING: Do not cook anything unless there is an adult to help you. Always ask an adult to do the cooking on a hot stove.

YOU WILL NEED
1/2 pound (225 g) broad egg noodles
3 eggs
1/2 pint (235 ml) of cottage cheese
1/2 pint (235 ml) sour cream
1/2 cup (120 ml) milk
1/2 cup (120 g) sugar
1/4 pound (110 g) melted butter or margarine
1/4 teaspoon cinnamon
1 teaspoon vanilla
corn flakes
1/2 cup (120 g) raisins

FOLLOW THE STEPS

1. Boil the noodles in a pot of water until they are soft. Drain the noodles.
2. Mix together all the ingredients except the noodles and corn flakes.
3. Add the noodles to the mixture.
4. Pour into a square buttered pan.
5. Sprinkle the top of the mixture with corn flakes.
6. Bake for one hour at 350 degrees Fahrenheit (175 degrees Centigrade).

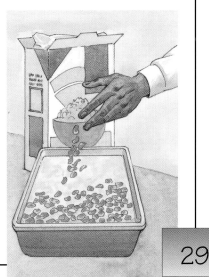

The New Americans

Slowly the **immigrants** felt more at home in the United States. They learned to speak English. They passed the test to become United States **citizens**. Their children became friends with children from other countries. They grew up to become America's teachers, doctors, and business leaders.

Immigrants still arrive in the United States today. Their foods, languages, and ideas have become part of American life.

ELLIS ISLAND MUSEUM

Ellis Island closed in 1954. Workers spent years cleaning and repairing it. They turned it into a museum that opened in 1990. Almost half the people in the United States today have relatives who passed through Ellis Island.

Glossary

citizen member of a country who has a right to live there

first class on a ship, the rooms that are the largest, cost the most money, and have the best service

government people who make laws and decisions for a country

immigrant someone who comes from another country to live in a new country

immigration center place where people who come into a country must answer questions and get permission to enter

inspector someone who checks things or asks questions

interpreter person who explains in one language what a person said in a different language

Native American one of the first people living in North America, Central America, and South America

oyster sea animal that has a soft body inside two shells that are hinged together

seasickness dizzy or sick to the stomach feeling some people get when on board a ship at sea

second class on a ship, the rooms that cost less than first class, but still have more comforts than steerage

steerage section of a ship for passengers paying the lowest fare

telegraph machine that sends messages over wires in the form of a code

More Books to Read

Owens, Thomas S. *Ellis Island.* New York: Rosen Publishing Group, 1997.

Young, Robert. *A Personal Tour of Ellis Island.* Minneapolis: Lerner Publishing Group, 2001.

Index